Power Thieves

7 Spirits that Steal your POWER
and How to Get it Back!

Edie Bayer

Power Thieves

ISBN: **978-0692211151**

DEDICATED

To Family:
I love you more than you will ever know.
But not as much as God!
He loves you too much
To leave you the way you are.

Power Thieves

CONTENTS

Power Thieves

Preface

When I was praying for a title for this book, the Lord asked me, "What do they all have in common?" At first I was stumped. I really didn't even know what He was saying. Was He talking about the chapters, the stories, the names of the spirits....?

He repeated the question, "What do all these spirits have in common?"

I thought about it. A lack of Humilty perhaps? That those persons infected with these spirits exhibit a definite lack of humility. I thought that perhaps without them one would be more humble? Then if one had more humility and God exalts the humble, then one would have more ....

POWER.

Then it hit me. They all steal power! They are all *POWER THIEVES*!

God said YES. These seven parasite spirits sap the life-power out of their hosts. Of course! And once rid of these thieves, any minister of the Gospel cannot help but have a power surge!

God is so smart.

This is even more amazing! The very last page of the first book that God gave me, Spiritual Espionage, lists these seven spirits. I didn't realize it until I was into the second or third chapter of this book. I'm just recording what God says. I write what I hear. I interject some stories from my own experiences with the Lord, but other than that it's straight from Him.

So, when God gave me the content for this book He said, "Write these down in the order I give you..." and then proceeded to give me the spirits' names listed in the order of the chapters ! It was absolutely amazing to me to discover that Jehovah Sneaky had done that!

Isn't that awesome?

I recommend you read each chapter and follow the steps at the end, including praying the prayers. Do not skip any of the chapters because even if you don't think you have an issue with that particular devil, they're pretty sly and they know how to hide. It won't hurt you to do it.

After all, God knew that you would be reading this book. He put these 7-power thieves in the first book because He knew that you would need this information. He has BIG plans for you! And to fulfill those goals and the Father's vision you will need more POWER. So, He wants to get that power to you, since He is your Source, your spiritual power plant, if you will. He knows what you need.

Now, let's get started. Take back your POWER!

1 Kings 19:1-2 (AMP)

19 Ahab told Jezebel all that Elijah had done and how he had slain all the prophets [of Baal] with the sword.
[2] Then Jezebel sent a messenger to Elijah, saying, So let the gods do to me, and more also, if I make not your life as the life of one of them by this time tomorrow.

Revelation 2:20-25 (AMP)

[20] But I have this against you: that you tolerate the woman Jezebel, who calls herself a prophetess [claiming to be inspired], and who is teaching and leading astray my servants *and* beguiling them into practicing sexual vice and eating food sacrificed to idols.
[21] I gave her time to repent, but she has no desire to repent of her immorality [symbolic of idolatry] *and* refuses to do so.
[22] Take note: I will throw her on a bed [[a]of anguish], and those who commit adultery with her [her paramours] I will bring down to [b]pressing distress *and* severe affliction, unless they turn away their minds from conduct [such as] hers *and* repent of [c]*their* doings.
[23] And I will strike her children (her proper followers) dead [thoroughly exterminating them]. And all the assemblies (churches) shall recognize *and* understand that I am He Who searches minds (the thoughts, feelings, and purposes) and the [inmost] hearts, and I will give to each of you [the reward for what you have done] as your work deserves.
[24] But to the rest of you in Thyatira, who do not hold this teaching, who have not explored *and* known the depths of Satan, as they

say—I tell you that I do not lay upon you any other [fresh] burden: ²⁵ Only hold fast to what you have until I come.

The First Power-Thief is the Jezebel Spirit.

I had a run-in with the Jezebel spirit that almost destroyed my life. As a direct result I really don't like her.

I was a single Mom living with my son in a run-down little 2-bedroom house, one of three that sat in the middle of 40-acres. My landlady lived next to me in a house that was bigger but even more run-down than mine, and there was an equally low-end duplex on the other side.

I will never forget this day. It was the day I went to war against Jezebel.

I was reading the book of Revelation, lounging in the sun, stretched out on a reclining patio chair. I remember I was so comfortable and happy. I had no work to do and my son was either playing video games or away with a friend. Either way it was quiet, the sun was shining and I was relaxed.

Life was good.

I was reading Revelation and Jesus was talking to His seven churches. The one that caught my attention was Revelation 2:20-25. Jesus was speaking to the church of Thyatira, and chastised them for their doings with this "woman" Jezebel, who promoted sexual immorality and eating things sacrificed to idols. This piqued my curiosity, because I remembered a certain Jezebel from another story who had been killed, and the dogs had lapped up her blood. I couldn't see how she could possibly still be around for Jesus to talk about at this church when she was already dead. Certainly some time had passed between the prophet Elijah's time and when John was imprisoned on Patmos?

Was this the same person? Or was there another Jezebel? And why was Jesus talking about her?

I set off on a crusade to find out as much as I could about Jezebel from a biblical perspective. It didn't take long until I figured out how bad she was for the church, for the body and that she was just all-around nasty. It turned out she was a self-proclaimed prophetess, a Queen who became the mistress of a cult of Baal worshipers who were promiscuous and adulterous. She also hated Elijah, because he had killed over 400 of her priests. She manipulated and controlled her husband King Ahab. She had a man killed for his land because the man wouldn't sell it to Ahab. She was mean, manipulative, controlling and vicious.

However, during my studies, I kept hearing about a *spirit* --- the Jezebel spirit. I was trying to link the two, this "woman" Jezebel and the "spirit" called Jezebel.

I found a couple of different theories. One theory held that the woman Jezebel gave her name to the spirit of Jezebel. The characteristics of her personality and the characteristics of this spirit were so similar people began to call this spirit the Jezebel spirit. The other theory was that this demonic spirit invaded the body of Jezebel, and that even after her death it lived on in her name, invading other humans as it required.

Regardless, the Jezebel spirit is the one that we are going to be dealing with here. The woman Jezebel is long dead and gone, but the spirit thrives. Not only in women, but in men too.

Jezebel Characteristics to consider:

Do you know anyone like this?

1. Controlling
2. Manipulative
3. Unsubmissive
4. Promiscuous
5. Hates Men (or women)
6. Rebels against authority

7. Lies
8. MUST always be right

There are a dozen other characteristics, but the ones with which I am most familiar are listed here.

That was ME once this spirit got a hold of me. I am sure you know others like this, too. Although I displayed some of the other characteristics at different times, I mostly exhibited the character traits of rebellion, unsubmissiveness, lust and always having to be right. And then it threw in a little control for good measure.

My troubles with Jezebel came about when I discovered that this spirit had infiltrated the church that I was attending. It was brought to my attention that this spirit was freely operating in my church, even though I didn't recognize it or realize it due to my spiritual immaturity. It could have been that the enemy blinded me to this fact deliberately or perhaps I may have already been infected with the Jezebel spirit myself. Whatever it was, I was completely clueless.

However, someone that I trusted in the church as a dear friend and knowledgeable about both these things and the people in the church had given me this information. I trusted this person, and had no reason to doubt the validity of the facts this person had imparted to me. My friend said that there had been an episode of sexual promiscuity in the church at high levels, and that even though that affair had been ended the church had never been "cleansed" of the spirit that motivated the actions.

That was all I needed to hear! Armed with baby faith and barely enough scripture to go to battle, I decided to conquer and banish this spirit and "cleanse" my church from this unwanted controller. In fact, I decided to cleanse the entire region, my beloved home state Texas. After all, it was just a spirit and 10:17 – 20 said that the spirits MUST submit to us in the Name of Jesus, right?

WHEW! The thing I DID NOT know was how high up the enemy-military ladder this particular spirit is. I didn't realize that taking on a powerful spirit with a high rank such as Jezebel would almost wreck my life. In hind-sight, I suppose that was the enemy's plan, to wreck my life with my own ignorance!

So, I set about doing exactly that, vanquishing this spirit. I started to pray and declare and decree and to rid my church and this area of the country of the pestilence of Jezebel. I did it all by myself. No prayer covering. I hadn't even bothered to clear it with my Pastor. I just made the decision to do it, and did.

MAJOR BLUNDER. Never, EVER attack a powerful spirit by yourself. Always have prayer covering, always do it as a group, ALWAYS have God on your side. Francis Frangipane's book on this topic will help you.

I hadn't even asked God if I should attempt it. I just did it.

I have learned since then that Jesus never did anything He did not see the Father doing. He never said anything He did not hear the Father saying. Jesus is our example. Did I hear the Father tell me to take on the spirit of Jezebel?

No.

The thing about the spirit of Jezebel is this – it doesn't care about your armor. It will invade through the cracks in your armor and will not run from you. It will find opportune areas in your life to entice you to sin and to "eat things offered to idols", invite you to be promiscuous and adulterous and be part of its cult. It will manipulate you, and control you. In turn, you manipulate and control others.

In short, it turns on you, it doesn't run. It embraces you and seduces you, it doesn't get mad. It just simply now knows you are there, and instead of killing you off it recruits you. Slowly. Deceptively. Seductively. In your attitudes and your actions, it presents "options" – CHOICES -- that seem logical and downright attractive.

At least at first.

Once it figures out it cannot have you it WILL try to kill you.

I think that had I left it alone, I would have been fine. Maybe it was a lesson the Lord WANTED me to learn. Perhaps, knowing that I would write this book one day, He WANTED me to get the word out to His people. It is said that you can only write about what you know. It's possible He wanted me to KNOW this spirit intimately, its implications and its characteristics, how it *feels* as well as what it *does* – and the ramifications of interacting with it from both sides of the fence.

The Jezebel spirit recruited me, too. I found myself fighting and gossiping, back stabbing and in short, not a nice person. I went out dancing and drinking with my church friends! In fact, I'd turned the church into my own personal social club, and most of the females in my age group were members. As a leader in the church, Jezebel's favorite target and its target of choice, I had access to everyone and everything there. Everyone knew me, giving me an unfair advantage. I drank and partied with the other girls I hung out with, all while I was a "respected" leader of a church.

Planning a pool party one day with a couple of my church girlfriends I actually remember saying something like, "If Pastor only knew that we live double lives!"

I think about that remark every now and then. That is the mark of the Jezebel spirit. It has two faces. It smiles at you and stabs you in the back. It manipulates and controls you by fear, intimidation, confusion and even abuse when necessary. Control is a Jezebel requirement because it must win every argument, because it must always be right. It sleeps around, but wears a mask of innocence and points fingers at others.

I remember hearing a message one Sunday at church by a visiting Pastor about immorality. I was so intensely convicted that I decided to change my ways.

That's when it got mad. See, it's like a rejected girlfriend. It will put sugar in your carburetor; it will throw battery acid on your car paint. It will affect your finances. It will invade your relationships in every area. There are no boundaries that it will not cross in your life to kill, steal and destroy you.

For two solid years I battled this spirit as it sought to wreck my life. It did everything but strangle me in my sleep.

My 12 year old son got brought home by the police one night, out walking in the ditches at midnight with his friends, all dressed in black. The sheriff who brought him home made him apologize to me, but it wasn't my son, really. It was the spirit.

I was busted at church for inappropriate activities. I had to step down from my leadership position. The one who busted me was one of the aforementioned pool party girlfriends! But that's just another facet of Jezebel's charming character.

My finances went VERY bad. The electricity at my house was almost disconnected multiple times and in fact one time the electric company truck was in the yard to shut off my power. I talked the driver into waiting until my mother showed up with some cash. My cell phone was shut off multiple times. I finally had to leave it shut off.

My ex-husband came and took his pickup truck in the early morning hours and left me stranded with a young son and no transportation.

The central air conditioner broke down at the little rundown house we occupied, so I had to use window air conditioner units to cool it, costing around 20% of my monthly income to keep it cool during our long, hot and humid Houston summers.

My little brother gave me an old Chevy Astro van. My son and I laughingly called it "La Bomba" because it was a JUNKER, truly a BOMB. It needed oil and transmission fluid every day just to run. It had no air conditioning, heat or defroster. But it was transportation and after going without anything to drive for a couple of weeks I was grateful! When I got another vehicle I gave "La Bomba" to one of the duplex residents next door who drove it with no plates and it ended up getting impounded.   My little brother got so mad at me, and rightfully so, because it was still in his name!

WHAT A NIGHTMARE!!

God kept sending help in different ways, but I was the one described in Haggai 1:6 with the holes in my money sack...it just wouldn't last and I couldn't cover all the bills. There were times I had to go without eating so my son could eat. We got to a point where I had to pay my rent every two weeks because I couldn't come up with the entire rent at the beginning of the month anymore.

God cannot bless sin. I had become willingly involved with this spirit. I had done it in ignorance, yes, but willingly nonetheless. I put myself in a position of danger, and this spirit had sucked me in.

I cried out to God for help. He is merciful, and He is just. I repented of my involvement with the spirit of Jezebel, and started to diligently re-apply Biblical principles to my life. As each situation arose in an area of my life that previously was ruled by the spirit of Jezebel, I was faced with a choice --- Did I want to continue behaving the way I was, or did I want change? I wanted to change. I wanted to please God and be obedient once again, to come under God's protection once more.

I made a determined effort by the power of the Holy Spirit to turn back the works of darkness. In other words, I CHOSE God.

I wish I could truthfully say that I am completely over the whole Jezebel thing. I would love to be able to report that there are no further struggles in my life as a result of doing business with this spirit. But I cannot. As situations come up, I still sometimes have to make the choice for God. Sometimes I fall. But ultimately, as my behavior patterns become more and more Godly, the situations become fewer and further apart. The blessings for obedience and adhering to a Godly behavior pattern far outweigh any momentary sense of fulfillment I might get by poor choices.

In time, the Lord blessed me with Darryl Bayer, who God has used mightily in my life both relationally and in ministry. He is my husband, my friend and my ministry partner. Darryl is a mighty man of God with a massive mantle for Kingdom business. We live on a really sweet parcel of land on a street of half-million dollar homes.

I have gone back to work part-time for Joan Hunter Ministries again, and am free to minister with our own ministry, Kingdom Promoters. I travel as a speaker and we host other speakers in our home.

My husband and I are getting ready to begin the Woodlands Symphony Orchestra, a lifetime dream of his.

I am writing books, a lifetime dream of my own. I am looking to get a horse, maybe two!

Life is good.

We have come full circle. Selah.

~~~~~~

Turn on Your Power, Shut Down the Power Thief Jezebel -- Key#1

Ask God for forgiveness. 1 John 1:9

If we confess our sins, he is faithful and just to forgive us *our* sins, and to cleanse us from all unrighteousness.

Repent of your involvement with the Jezebel Spirit. Acts 3:19

So repent (change your mind and purpose); turn around *and* return [to God], that your sins may be erased (blotted out, wiped clean), that times of refreshing (of recovering from the effects of heat, of [a]reviving with fresh air) may come from the presence of the Lord;

Apply Biblical principles to life situations. 2 Peter 3:18

But grow in grace, and [in] the knowledge of our Lord and Saviour Jesus Christ. To him [be] glory both now and forever.

When faced with choices, CHOOSE LIFE. Deuteronomy 30:19

Today I have given you the choice between life and death, between blessings and curses. Now I call on heaven and earth to witness the choice you make. Oh, that you would choose life, so that you and your descendants might live!

Prayer: Dear Jesus, I repent of my involvement with the Jezebel spirit. Lord, I repent of every act of treachery which I performed under the bewitchment of Jezebel. Lord from this day forward I CHOOSE LIFE! I choose to walk with You! Lord, I refuse to accept any guidance or wisdom from any other spirit other than the Holy Spirit of God, in Jesus' Name! Father, thank You for Your forgiveness! In Jesus' Name, Amen

Isaiah 43:18-19 (NIV)
"Forget the former things;
do not dwell on the past.

See, I am doing a new thing!
Now it springs up; do you not perceive it?
I am making a way in the desert
and streams in the wasteland."

The second Power Thief is "Demons of the Past". Some people are stuck in the past because of violence and abuse; some because their memories of the past are better than what they are currently experiencing.

Getting over the past was one of the hardest things I have ever had to do. It seems as if rose-colored glasses come standard equipment! At least for some people. I was one of them.

I never WANTED to get hung up on the past. It just seemed to happen. But since God either ALLOWS things to happen or CAUSES them….it must have been Him. And it must be such a common occurrence that God wants me to share how I got over it, so you can too!

You know the old saying, "God never wastes anything"? A good example is to look at the 3-fishes and 5-loaves, whereby the Lord sent the disciples out to pick up the crumbs and pieces and put them into 12 baskets. The Bible doesn't indicate what happened to them afterward, but I am sure somebody ate them! God did not let those crumbs go to waste.

The broken pieces of our lives are the same. He will use them to minister to someone else effectively. God would not allow us to go through all the hurt, pain and suffering unless He had a good place to store all those tears. We know that He does, in His bottle (Psalm 56:8).

I want to preface this by saying that I am happily married to a wonderful man with whom I co-minister. You all know him, and if you don't you should! He is Darryl Bayer, the awesomely anointed trumpet player. Darryl and I have been married for several years now, and we knew each other for a year and a half before we got married.

That being said, I had a life before I met Darryl Bayer. Not all of it was bad. I intentionally tried to focus on those areas that were good memories, rather than focusing on the negative aspects of my previous relationships. This allowed me to walk in forgiveness and avoid bitterness and all the physical symptoms that accompany it.

But a lot of people simply get STUCK there! I was one of them for a while. You may know someone like this, or even have a story similar to one below.

1. Years ago there was a girl at church that I met who was still in love with a prior boyfriend, even though she was married to someone else entirely and had been for a number of years.
2. I know another woman who still lives in the 1970's. She idolizes all the old rock bands and singers from that era. In fact, her social media profile picture is a singer from a popular band from this era. She just simply never moved forward. She is STUCK in the 70's.
3. I know of a man who never got over his ex-wife. For years he would contact her on her birthday, and on the anniversary of their wedding date, even though they had been divorced for years. When she stopped receiving his phone calls, he continued to call her relatives and leave voicemail messages on their phones. He still occasionally sends email.

4. Another young lady makes a circuit of all her old boyfriends. She will be with one for a while, then will reminisce about another and rekindle the relationship with him. After a little while she becomes disenchanted with that one, contacts another and will leave the one she is with to go back to him. Then a while later, she does the same with another old boyfriend. And the cycle continues, on and on, recycling relationships.

5. I know of another man who also continued to harass his ex-wife constantly – when he drank. He would get drunk and get on the phone and berate her, curse her and try to shame her. She felt sorry for him and allowed it to happen. He just never got past their divorce.

Once I met that first lady, I determined to NEVER be a woman who was totally hung up on her past! BUT GOD....how rich is He in his mercy. He made me go through it anyway. God only allows us to go through trials because He will use that experience down the road for us to minister to someone else.

One quick story about my son's father to illustrate. We were divorced in 2004. We attempted at least four to five times to reconcile. However, by 2007 I had exited the world and its ways and was growing into a God-fearing woman. Conversely, he had stayed pretty much the same, still drinking and smoking and, well....doing the same stuff. After all as Creflo Dollar says, "Sinners Sin!" The Lord revealed in prayer to me one night that I was not in love with the man that I married anymore. I was in love with the MEMORY of what once was. That was critical information and a pivotal point to set me free!

The Israelites did it, too. They were so completely stuck in the past they were willing to return to slavery! We all know the story in the book of Exodus, how they berated Moses for dragging them out to the desert to die. They said they would have been better off in Egypt as slaves, at least there they had "**pots of food**" and lots of bread to eat (Ex. 16:3). Again, in Numbers 11:5 the Israelites reconfirmed their desire to live in the past, stating, **"We remember the fish we used to eat for free in Egypt. And we had all the cucumbers, melons, leeks, onions, and garlic we wanted."** (NLT)

Another example is Orpah, Ruth's sister-in-law. She was bound to the past. She couldn't go into an unknown future with Ruth and Naomi. She required the comfort of the past, the things she already knew – her family, her friends, her people-- and her gods. When Naomi originally bid the two women go back to Moab, she kissed them. This was more than a good-bye kiss. Naomi was "breathing" on them for the journey, imparting some of her own strength into them. When Orpah left the other two women to go back to Moab, she again kissed Naomi, in effect returning to her the "breath" that Naomi had given her. She wanted nothing to do with Naomi's people, or her God. She wanted her old comfort-zone.

My story of how I overcame the demons of the past will help you do it, too. Additionally, it will give you the basics to minister to others that need to be set free of this same bondage.

I had met someone a couple of years before I met Darryl. We both volunteered at the local healing room. He was in the process of a divorce, and was seeking counseling from one of the healing room administrators. My season of volunteering at the healing room only lasted for a few months, and it seemed that he was never there when I was there. However, we did talk a couple times, enough for me to start to like him. But since he was technically still married it was "hands-off" anyway, so I never really expected it to go anywhere. Time passed, I stopped volunteering at the Healing Room, and soon forgot about him.

Fast forward a couple of years, and I was at church with my Mother and Dad on Father's Day. My mother told me that this man attended their church, and he had asked about me several times when talking to them. It was quickly apparent he hadn't forgotten about me at all. He walked right up to me at the beginning of the service and we talked for a few minutes, during which agreed to go out sometime. A week or so later, I gave my mom my business card with some times to go see a movie on the back, and asked her to give it to him. She did, but I never heard anything back from him. Once again, I moved on with my life.

Months later it was New Years Eve. The same church from Father's Day was around the corner from my house. They were showing a movie, and I had the option of either going to see this movie on New Year's Eve or driving 30-miles to attend a service where Ras Robinson was speaking. I opted to go to the movie and avoid all the New Year's Eve revelry and accompanying drunk drivers.

Once again, he was there. He came up and sat beside me. We talked all the way through the movie. In fact, we talked so much that it caused his Pastor to turn around and look at us a couple of times. We really hit it off. I started to attend his church, and to spend time with him. I liked his Pastor anyway, and the church was right up my alley with solid doctrine and good teaching. It was a win-win in my books.

After a few months of dating this man, I allowed my brain to "go there" - Marriage. He seemed to me to be the perfect candidate for a husband. He was tall and handsome, lived on 11 acres and had horses. He was in construction and owned rental real estate. He wasn't wealthy, but had his own Air Conditioning company. We had lots of things in common, most importantly Jesus and foundational beliefs, and I fell head over heels for him. I really believed he was the one! He even took me to meet his mother.

Ironically, he was another person who was hung up on his past. After a while he confessed to me that he was still in love with his ex-wife. That really put a damper on my plans! I had to make the hard decision to break up with him, because there just really was no point in taking a back seat to a woman who he still loved – divorced or not.

I had met Darryl about a year or so before that New Year's Eve movie. Darryl and I had seen each other off-and-on, and we were not seeing each other during the time I was seeing the other gentleman. After I broke up with this man, Darryl sent me an email one night, and the rest is history. Darryl won me over, and asked me to marry him. I did.

But my feelings for the other man didn't magically disappear just because he was no longer in my life. I had really fallen for him, and found myself in the position of being married to one man whom I loved and having feelings for another man – in my past -- at the same time. It tore me to pieces daily! I didn't know if I had made the right choice. What if I had married the wrong man? What if I should have waited for him to come around? What if, what if...?

After a year or so of being tormented with these thoughts, miserable and making Darryl miserable, I went to the Lord. I cried out to Him to take the memories away of the other man. I cried out to God to erase the feelings and the thoughts that I had for him. I said to God, "If you want me to be happily married with Darryl, you HAVE to remove all the memories and feelings that I feel for this other person!"

That did it. It took a few more weeks, and more crying out to God for the erasure, but the thoughts became fewer and further apart, and the feelings disappeared completely. It was not an immediate healing, I still had to walk it out. I was cleansed of the demons of the past as I went, just like the lepers in Luke 17:14.

I know, I should have done that first, right? Well, I'm human. It didn't really ever occur to me to go to God and ask Him to do it.

How simple was that?

In the process, I learned that
1) I had to cry out to God to save me, and
2) I had to trust Him to do it.
It was nothing that I did or could have done – I had to trust HIM to do it for me.

But once again, God is so rich in His mercy that He allowed me to walk out this miserable existence, which was grossly unfair to my husband

and made me completely hateful and intolerable, both angry and resentful. The good news was that this situation enabled me to be able to minister *effectively* to those that are caught in the same snare as I was --- caught in the snare of the past.

As a bonus I wound up realizing through multiple prayer sessions of crying out to God that my covenant is with HIM. I am married to Darryl, but my marriage covenant is truly with Him, Father God. That one revelation is the glue that held all the shattered pieces of my existence together during those tough months. Not wanting to break covenant with God caused me to be able to stay married to Darryl.

Please understand I am being transparent here! I was in a trial, deceived by the enemy, who wanted me powerless and licking my wounds in the corner. The enemy wanted me to focus on *what used to be* (the past), unable to move forward with my assignment and my life.

Well, that didn't happen! I am happily married to a great guy, a fabulous husband, an amazing ministry partner and an equally amazing father to my son and son to my parents. I love him and am BLESSED to have him!

Darryl was then, too. I just couldn't see it through the clogged filter of my heart pain.

Which is exactly where the enemy wants us. He WANTS us to be oblivious to anyone else other than ourselves. He WANTS us to have those divisive thoughts of divorce and strife. He doesn't want us to turn to God our Father for salvation! Yet, that is exactly what it will take, if you or someone you love is going through a struggle like I did, one of being chained to the past.

Set yourself and others free. Take your focus off yourself, and encourage them to do the same. Do what is right. Go to God. It's easy and it's FREE. He has all the answers. He is not a "hidden" God, as a spiritual mentor of mine would say. He will answer your questions and send help when you need it – if you only open your mouth and ask.

~~~~~~

Turn Your Power On, Shut Down the Power Thief "Demons of The Past"
– Key #2

1. Realize that the enemy of your soul is at work. It is his minions that are running rampant in your life. Realize the enemy is working on you, taking your FOCUS off of Jesus and Kingdom business and putting it on you.
2. Now, take Your Focus off yourself. Allowing the Demons of the Past to rule in your life is SELF-ish – you are focusing on your SELF. The only way to get your focus off of YOU is to turn your focus outward. Turn your focus back onto Jesus, and onto other people. Minister to others. Pray for them. Serve them in some way that makes you think of THEIR NEEDS and not your own. Keep doing it.
3. Go to God. Actually, you should do this FIRST! Just as I learned that if I ask God for help He will gladly help me, He will help you, too. Cry out to Him! Ask Him for His will to be done in your life. Don't spend another minute in misery.
4. Repent
5. Pray and be specific. Ask Him to remove specific memories of specific people and/or specific actions. He will do it. He will give you an entirely new film reel from which to draw your memories if you ask Him.
6. It is the Father's good pleasure to give you the Kingdom. Begin today.

Ask God for forgiveness. 1 John 1:9

If we confess our sins, he is faithful and just to forgive us *our* sins, and to cleanse us from all unrighteousness.

Repent of dissatisfaction and wasting time. Acts 3:19

So repent (change your mind and purpose); turn around *and* return [to God], that your sins may be erased (blotted out, wiped clean), that times of refreshing (of recovering from the effects of heat, of [a]reviving with fresh air) may come from the presence of the Lord;

Prayer: Lord, I repent of my dissatisfaction with my present day life. Thank you for your forgiveness. Please help me to move forward with both my life and my assignment. I repent of wasting time and living in the past. I want to be in the present, with You, moving toward my future. Lord Jesus, please erase the memories of (_____). Take away the pain of (_____). Allow me to fully LIVE in the moment, Lord. Thank you for giving me all new memories. Thank you for LIFE, and LIFE more abundantly (John 10:10)! Thank you Lord. In Jesus' Name. Amen.

EDIE BAYER

Proverbs 6:16-19 (AMP)

[16] These six things the Lord hates, indeed, seven are an abomination to Him:
[17] A proud look [the spirit that makes one overestimate himself and underestimate others], a lying tongue, and hands that shed innocent blood,
[18] A heart that manufactures wicked thoughts *and* plans, feet that are swift in running to evil,
[19] A false witness who breathes out lies [even under oath], and he who sows discord among his brethren.

The third Power Thief is Pride.

The Spirit of Pride is a major problem, a growing one, both globally and here in this country. Many seem to have a spirit of entitlement, which is Pride on steroids, but that is fodder for another book!

Pride is something that God DESPISES, according to Proverbs 6:16-19.

Yet how many of us walk with a spirit of pride in us? I know I have. I consistently continue to repent of pride, prayerfully as soon as I catch it! Sadly, like bad breath, we are usually the last to know that we have it. Pride is like tar, it is sticky. It's ugly and black. And it gets all over other people. It's contagious. And it is potentially lethal.

I have learned that if we don't quickly repent of pride, that God will humble us. Why? Because He opposes the proud but He gives grace to the humble. God has made sure I have had incidents that humbled me. God said that "Pride goes before destruction, and a haughty spirit before a fall" (Proverbs 16:18). Well, I have fallen alright. Many times.

I remember hearing a message by Bill Johnson once about a plant on his desk. It started to drop its leaves until it was just a stick in the pot. He said that God told him that plant was him! God was going to strip him until he looked like that plant.

That was me, too. God stripped away every crutch, every excuse, every shred of pride I had. I remember one time I was so mad at God! I was a single mom, and self employed. My business had slowed down A LOT, and it had gotten longer and longer between paychecks. On this particular occasion I was waiting, and waiting, and waiting for a paycheck to come. Day after day I waited. Now, I am not a patient person in the natural! I got so tired of the pressure, so tired of being broke and so tired of waiting that I became a blubbering mess on the floor of my office, shaking my finger in God's face, telling Him *I had HAD IT! I was DONE! I was going back to being a bartender, at least then I knew I'd make some money! I'd HAD IT with this Christian life.*

Can you just HEAR the pride and arrogance? Yuk.

Of course, I didn't quit. I didn't go back to the bar. God came through at 11:59. In fact it might have been closer to 12:00. But He came through. He ALWAYS does! Later I apologized to the Lord.

And that is how I ended up in the ministry, incidentally. God stripped away every fiber of pride that I had in my life. He took away everything that I had learned to lean on, including my business and my friends. He even took away my truck!! Of course He provided another one eventually, but not until I learned to depend on him. He had to strip me of my dependence on myself, and on the spirit of pride, before I would lean fully on him.

 Anyway, I used to roll my eyes in unbelief at the income people made in the church. I was a mortgage broker, and a prideful one at that, making a 6-figure annual income. My typical response was, "SERIOUSLY! And you LIVE on that??? There is NO WAY EVER that you would catch me dead working for that kind of money!"

Actually I was right. I got saved! Again. This time from myself.

Plus, no matter how hard I kicked against the goads, God had already decided otherwise. He stripped me of that foolish pride, too, and sure enough, I wound up working for Joan Hunter Ministries. I started out as an independent contractor working in the warehouse, moving boxes, and glad to do it. I remember those hard days of needing the money so badly. Later I was hired on full time, and moved up the ladder to become Joan's events coordinator. From there I went to work with Paulette Reed and Prophetic Arrow Ministries, and now my husband and I are stewarding Kingdom Promoters, another ministry for the Lord.

And loving it!

Here's the thing...God takes away pride for our own good benefit. Had I had my own ignorant way, I would NEVER have gone into the ministry. And I would have missed out on the most fulfilling, enjoyable, soul-satisfying experiences and Holy Ghost adventures imaginable this side of eternity. I am so grateful to God that He put me in ministry.

Pride is sin. Sin separates us from God. God takes sin out of us, by whatever means necessary. I heard once that God either CAUSES things, or ALLOWS them. Either way, it's for His Glory.

So, that's the preamble. This is the promise:

God will do it to YOU, too! And For you. And through you!

Yes, He will use you to humble others as well. My mother used to say that sometimes she needed to *"knock me down off my high horse"*, an old Scottish saying meaning to "take me down a peg or two". That is exactly what God does. He uses other people to do His will, to humble them, so later He can exalt them!

As an example, once I was ushering at my church. There was a man drinking a soda in the church sanctuary – a BIG ONE in a GREAT BIG

WHITE STYROFOAM CUP, the kind you really can't miss. It was part of my job description as an usher to maintain the sanctuary, cleaning, straightening chairs, and enforcing the rules. Our rules were the same as most other churches about having food and drinks in the sanctuary. There were signs posted that said NO FOOD OR DRINKS allowed, so it seemed to be pretty straightforward. Anyway, this man was married to someone that was a part of the church leadership. When I said something to him, and told him he would have to take his soda out to the lobby and pick it up later, he was VERY offended.

The rules were the same for him as they were for everyone else in the church. However, he didn't think so. Part of God's plan is to respect authority, because all authority is given by God. I had the authority to ask him to do something because God gave it to me. He didn't respect that authority, and became offended instead of submitting.

He had a spirit of PRIDE, plain and simple. He got up and walked out of the church, and took his soda with him. He didn't come back to the church for months because of a soft drink. Tell ME that's not the enemy! A spirit of pride successfully routed this man from the church, from fellowship, from teaching and from worshiping the ONE TRUE GOD.... all because of a soda pop.

However, in his defense, he did have a valid point. He said during our conversation that the Pastor's wife always had big cups of soda (or tea or coffee) by her seat all the time. He was right. Thankfully the head usher agreed with me, that ALL church members (including ALL Leadership and spouses, children, etc.) had to abide by the rules. At least there was no backlash from him. Pastor's wife wasn't too happy! But that's another story.

And what about Job? In Job Chapter 41, v. 34, God Says (speaking of Leviathan), "[34] He looks all mighty [beasts of prey] in the face [without terror]; he is monarch over all the sons of pride. And now, Job, [a]who are you who dares not arouse the unmastered crocodile, yet who dares resist Me, the beast's Creator, to My face?

Everything under the heavens is Mine; therefore, who can have a claim against God?"

God resists the proud! In Chapter 42 Job repented of speaking out **against the Lord. A little later,** in verse 7, it is recorded that his friend Eliphaz had made God angry. Job had to pray for him to save him from the wrath of God! Talk about humbling! That will bring you down "off your high horse"!

"7 After the Lord had spoken the previous words to Job, the Lord said to Eliphaz the Temanite, My wrath is kindled against you and against your two friends, for you have not spoken of Me the thing that is right, as My servant Job has.

8 Now therefore take seven bullocks and seven rams and go to My servant Job and offer up for yourselves a burnt offering; and My servant Job shall pray for you, for I will accept [his prayer] that I deal not with you after your folly, in that you have not spoken of Me the thing that is right, as My servant Job has.

9 So Eliphaz the Temanite and Bildad the Shuhite and Zophar the Naamathite went and did as the Lord commanded them; and the Lord accepted [Job's prayer]." (Job 42:7-9, AMP)

Sometimes God will throw a two-fer at you such as he did at Job. Job and his three friends were ALL humbled at one time. The Lord did the same thing to me once. I had borrowed a flat iron (a "Chi", to those in the know!) from one of the ladies I worked with at the ministry. During the course of using it, I had gotten some excess "product" into the edges of the iron, and making it sticky and not very attractive and the Teflon coating on the blades had gotten scratched. I returned the iron, and the gal I had borrowed it from was NOT happy about the condition it was in.

I bought another flat iron for her. She didn't ask me to do it. I simply valued her friendship more than a $100 flat iron. And when I gave her the brand new, pretty pink flat iron that I bought I told her so, too.

She was humbled, and so was I. I learned the value of a friendship, and taking care of something that was loaned to me (think about the axe head that was lost in the Jordan in 2 Kings 6, the one that floated to the surface). She was humbled that I spent $100 to replace the "Chi", knowing that as a single mom with almost NO extra money (which is why I borrowed it to begin with!) that her friendship was more of a priority to me than the cost of a flat iron.

I never asked her about it again, but I would guess she was pretty happy with it. Her hair sure looked good!

~~~~~~

Turn Your Power On, Shut Down the Power Thief "Pride" – Key #3

Ask God for forgiveness. 1 John 1:9

If we confess our sins, he is faithful and just to forgive us *our* sins, and to cleanse us from all unrighteousness.

Repent of your involvement with the spirit of Pride. Acts 3:19

So repent (change your mind and purpose); turn around *and* return [to God], that your sins may be erased (blotted out, wiped clean), that times of refreshing (of recovering from the effects of heat, of [a]reviving with fresh air) may come from the presence of the Lord;

Command the spirit of Pride to go. Luke 10:17

Then the seventy[c] returned with joy, saying, "Lord, even the demons are subject to us in Your name."

The Keys to getting rid of Pride are simple.

1. Repent for coming into agreement with the spirit of pride.
2. Cut the spirit of pride off of your life.

3. Command it to go and to never return.
4. Ask Holy Spirit to fill up the places that the spirit of pride had previously occupied.

Prayer: "Lord, I repent for coming into agreement with the spirit of pride and for having any involvement with it. In the Name of Jesus I cut the spirit of pride off of my life. In the Name of Jesus I command the spirit of pride to go now and to never return. Lord, in Jesus' Name I thank you that it is finished, and I thank You for Your forgiveness. Holy Spirit come fill me now, fill me up and fill up all the empty places that the spirit of pride had previously occupied. Jesus, breathe on me anew. Fill me with breath and spirit, Your breath and Spirit. Thank you Jesus."

EDIE BAYER

1 Samuel 15:23 (NKJV)

"For rebellion *is as* the sin of witchcraft,
And stubbornness *is as* iniquity and idolatry.
Because you have rejected the word of the LORD,
He also has rejected you from *being* king."

The fourth Power Thief is Rebellion.

Webster's 1828 Dictionary defines REBELLION this way: "Open resistance to lawful authority."

A more apt definition for the spiritual side of rebellion is this one by Noah Webster in speaking of the Romans: "...rebellion was originally a revolt or open resistance to their government by nations that had been subdued in war. *It was a renewed war.*"

If we consider that the dark side of the spiritual realm has already been subdued then this is truly what the spirit of rebellion is --- *A renewing of a war that has already been won by Jesus.* "Stripping the rulers and authorities of their power, he made a public spectacle of them, triumphing over them by means of the stake." (Col. 2:15, Complete Jewish Bible)

We typically think of James Dean, *the rebel without a cause*, or "rebellious teenagers" when we think of rebellion. But rebellion can take many forms, and it is a "Power Thief".

1. How many cigarette smokers do you know? Cigarette smoking is typically a symptom of rebellion.
2. How many people do you know that are "living together"? Pre-marital sex, same sex marriage and all types of sexual perversion including homosexuality and its twins, Lesbianism and Transexuality are symptoms of rebellion.
3. Know anyone who has been divorced? Or are YOU a divorcee? Divorce, or its typical precursor infidelity are symptoms.
4. Are you habitually late to meetings and church? Even something as seemingly innocuous as being late to work or taking a "long lunch" without permission is a symptom of rebellion.
5. Not paying ones bills on time is definitely a symptom of rebellion.
6. Complaining is rebellion in every instance.

There are thousands of different ways that rebellion can manifest, as many as there are people to rebel. However, at the root of every public issue is a more private one – disobedience to God. If we are obedient to God, then there is no rebellion. If we are obedient to God, then we do not behave in ways that manifest in civil detriment.

Rebellion and disobedience are so closely related that one cannot exist without the other. It is impossible to be in open rebellion without being disobedient. At the same time, a person (or spirit) must rebel against God (or His authority) in order to willingly be disobedient. Of course one can be disobedient without being in rebellion (i.e., running a stop sign we didn't see). However, for the sake of this discussion we are talking about willingly being rebellious.

We have glorified rebellion in the United States because our country was founded on it, independence, FREEDOM and all that goes with revolting against the British Government. But we cannot overlook the fact that in a revolution one must REVOLT against another's authority hence the name, Revolutionary War!

Let's look at cigarette smoking. This is a great example of rebellious behavior. If you know anyone who smokes, typically they started when they were very young, pre-teen or teenager. Personally, I started smoking at age 18. My son's father started at age 7!

Why do people take up smoking? You guessed it -- because their parents told them they couldn't, out of sheer rebellion! Smoking, as glamorous as it is, was for "adults only" or "off limits" or "when you are old enough" or "when you are living in your own house" or any one of a million things that parents say to attempt dissuade their young and assuage their own consciences. However, children are led by example and will do as you do and not as you say. If you smoke, you can be sure your children will as well.

Rebellion is the symptom of disobedience. Your child says to himself, "What? That's hypocrisy! They can do it but I can't? (Sounds like the snake in the garden talking to Eve, doesn't it?) Well, I'll show THEM!" and s/he takes that first painful puff of toxic chemicals laced with addictive additives into their lungs. They hack, and choke, because they have never experienced this inpouring of putrid air into their lungs before. But either peer pressure or the light-headedness they experience with this first cigarette prod them to go forward and do it again. This scene typically takes place around the back side of the garage, or out at the creek, or in a group in someone's back yard or at the park.

Your child will NEVER smoke in front of you, and if you are a smoker, they know you will not be able to smell it on them. So they think they have tricked you. They think they are smarter than you. They believed a lie, the same lie that was told to Eve at the fall, " For God knows that in the day you eat of it your eyes will be opened, and you will be like God..." (Gen. 3:5, Amp.) So now they believe they are "all grown up" and the true problems begin. The rebellion continues to escalate in a lot of cases, moving from cigarettes to alcohol or marijuana, marijuana to speed or cocaine or ecstasy or whatever the "drug du jour" might be for your child's generation.   Not in every case, of course. However, I have seen a lot of escalation happen in people's lives.

The root of rebellion is disobedience. The actual ACT that is performed – children born out of wedlock, unmarried and living together, being late to work, unpaid parking tickets, STD's, AIDS --- is simply a symptom of the larger problem.

When ones immune system is failing, there are multiple symptoms, from flu to cancer. Is the FLU the primary problem? No. The Flu is a symptom of a larger problem, that of the immune system failing, and so is the cancer. Of course, in our generation, this is really a symptom of a MUCH LARGER problem, which is rebellion resulting from disobedience. A lot of people contract HIV from a sexual partner, and it is generally NOT his or her spouse. Not in every case, of course, but we are all aware of the statistics that HIV carry with regard to the sexually promiscuous and especially homosexuals. Selah.

The same can be said for every form of disobedience, whether it is using foul language or simply refusing to comply with the direct order of your employer. The language is just a symptom, because the Bible is very clear in the directive, "Don't use foul or abusive language." (Eph. 4:29, NLT) When one uses foul language, s/he is in rebellion to the laws of God by being disobedient to the instruction. There is a Bible verse that covers every situation, and those that fail to live by the Word of God are in disobedience. Even not reading the Bible is disobedience! Joshua 1:8, ESV says, "This Book of the Law shall not depart from your mouth, but you shall meditate on it day and night, so that you may be careful to do according to all that is written in it. For then you will make your way prosperous, and then you will have good success."

The Word says about itself that "...you SHALL meditate on it day and night..." It does not imply that you might want to consider reading it. It does not say if you are not too tired or busy it might be ok to pick it up every once in a great while on Christmas and Easter. It doesn't say that. It says **YOU SHALL**. This is a direct order from God. When you do not comply with the "you shall" scriptures you are disobedient and subsequently in rebellion.

Later, the Word says in 2 Timothy 2:15 (AMP), "Study *and* be eager *and* do your utmost to present yourself to God approved (tested by trial), a workman who has no cause to be ashamed, correctly analyzing *and* accurately dividing [rightly handling and skillfully teaching] the Word of Truth." The Word says to STUDY THE WORD. If you do not wish to be approved, do not study the Word. You will be in disobedience, rebellious, and dis-approved!

Now that we have a foundation established from which to operate, I want you to look again at our flagship scripture from **1 Samuel 15:23** (NKJV)

"For rebellion *is as* the sin of witchcraft,
And stubbornness *is as* iniquity and idolatry.
Because you have rejected the word of the LORD,
He also has rejected you from *being* king."

Now, the story here of course is that Samuel the prophet has come back to the camp of Saul and found him with a live captured king and a bunch of animals – of which ALL were ordered to be slaughtered and NONE were ordered to be saved.   Saul gave him an excuse, but the truth eventually came out, that Saul caved in to public opinion rather than carrying out the Word of the Lord. He had a *"fear of man"* rather than a *"fear of the Lord"*.

The Fear of the Lord is the beginning of wisdom. Not the fear of man. (Proverbs 9:10)

The Amalekite king embodies in Hebrew *"lo yareh HaShem"* which is the lack of the fear of the Lord, and represents the power of darkness and evil in the world.   Instead of killing him, as God had instructed, Saul kept him alive out of TRADITION. The tradition of that period was to parade around with the captive king and his belongings, the spoils of war, displaying the battle victory for all to see. God was not interested in this display, the traditions of man. He wanted that king dead, out of Saul's life forever. But Saul refused. He was in rebellion.

When you are disobedient to the Word of God and in rebellion, this is YOU. You have a live king, one that is other than King Jesus. You have kept alive a king of darkness in your soul --- the spirit of rebellion, the spirit of the world.

{Author's Note: Just so you know you are not being "PREACHED AT" by my "holier than thou" attitude, the Holy Spirit is scrubbing me too. My heart hurts as this stinging essay goes on! I am being spiritually SANDED right along with you! He is speaking and I am just typing the words. The Holy Spirit is leading me and guiding me into all truth right

41

along with you (John 16:13). I am being cleansed and set free simultaneously right along with you. I knew there was a reason He picked these seven topics for me to write about! Every one of them I needed work on. And so do you! That is why He got this book into your hands. So we are in this thing together!}

What are the ramifications of having this "other king" around? It means that you have rejected the Word of the Lord, and He has NO CHOICE but to reject you as king. Put another way, it means that as long as you continue to be disobedient, continue to bow to the prince of this world, the prince of the air, the prince of darkness in your soul, that you do not qualify to be a king in God's Kingdom here in this earth realm.

Even if you are *almost* obedient, you are still in disobedience. Saul was *almost* all the way obedient. He killed off some of the people and kept the choicest animals to sacrifice to the Lord. His instructions were to slaughter ALL OF THEM, men, women, children and animals.

Isn't it enough to obey *ALMOST* all of the Bible?

There is a Kingdom of God and there is a Kingdom of Heaven. If you don't believe me, read the Bible and pay particular attention to how Jesus uses these phrases. They are NOT interchangeable, as you may have been taught to believe. The Kingdom of God is here on the earth, because Jesus says "...the Kingdom of God is within you." (Luke 17:21, KJV) The Kingdom of Heaven is where we are headed, or technically, where we are right now simultaneously on the earth and at the right hand of Christ Jesus.

In order to be a king here on the earth, you must (MUST) be subject to the King. That means that Jesus is your Lord and Savior. He is already your Savior. That is what HE did for you. Is He your Lord? This is something that you must do for HIM.

That means does He reign and rule in every part of your life, or just when it's convenient? Do you give Him permission to rule your tongue? Your mind? Your eyes? Your ears? He must rule over EVERY part of your life, including your thought life and the intents of your heart. He MUST be the filter of choice for every decision you make.

Do you hear me? The filter OF CHOICE. You must CHOOSE to allow Him to filter your music, your food, your computer, your television programs and movies you watch. You must CHOOSE to allow Him to filter your thoughts and words, your actions and your intentions.

James 4:4 says, "You adulteresses, do you not know that friendship with the world is hostility toward God? Therefore whoever wishes to be a friend of the world makes himself an enemy of God...." (NLT)

If you endeavor to keep the Amalekite king alive in your life, you will never be able to be a friend of God, a TRUE friend, a son and a king in the earth. Again, the Bible is pretty clear that if you love the world you hate Him, Jesus. If you are walking with the world, you are NOT walking in unity with Jesus. You are in rebellion and acting disobediently.

Do you want true power? Do you want to move in miracles, signs and wonders in the earth? Do you want to influence non-believers with Holy Ghost Power as Paul did (1 Cor. 2:4-5)? It's simple. Hack the Amalekite king to pieces like Samuel!

In 1 Samuel 15:32-33 (NKJV), "Then Samuel said, "Bring Agag king of the Amalekites here to me." So Agag came to him cautiously.

And Agag said, "Surely the bitterness of death is past."

[33] But Samuel said, "As your sword has made women childless, so shall your mother be childless among women." And Samuel hacked Agag in pieces before the LORD in Gilgal.

This is a picture of the Holy Spirit carrying out the orders of the Lord. Samuel did what the Lord told Saul to do. Since you cannot, in the natural, hack the prince of the world to pieces, you will need to do it in the spiritual realm. Samuel used a sword to cut up the Amalekite king. You can do the same. Pick up your Sword of the Spirit which is the Word of God!

Here is your prayer, based on scripture. Read it aloud, believe as a little child, and pick up your sword to cut off the head and hack the demons to pieces. It will feel good! You will be free!

Turn Your Power On, Shut Down the Power Thief "Rebellion" – Key #4

Ask God for forgiveness. 1 John 1:9

If we confess our sins, he is faithful and just to forgive us *our* sins, and to cleanse us from all unrighteousness.

Repent of your involvement with the spirit of Rebellion. Acts 3:19

So repent (change your mind and purpose); turn around *and* return [to God], that your sins may be erased (blotted out, wiped clean), that times of refreshing (of recovering from the effects of heat, of [a]reviving with fresh air) may come from the presence of the Lord;

Command the Demons to go. Luke 10:17

Then the seventy[e] returned with joy, saying, "Lord, even the demons are subject to us in Your name."

1. First of all Repent of your involvement with the spirit of Rebellion
2. Command the spirit of Rebellion to go and not return
3. Ask Holy Spirit to come and fill up those now-vacant spaces
4. Kill the king that has taken the place of King Jesus

Prayer: "Lord, I want to walk as a king, with the authority and the power of a heavenly king in the earth realm. Father, You said that if I reject your Word that You have no choice but to reject me as king. You cannot bless sin. It is sin for me to have a relationship with the prince of darkness by allowing the spirit of rebellion and spirit of disobedience to reside in my life. Lord, I take up the Sword of the Spirit, and I cut off the head of the spirit of rebellion in my life. Lord, I hack it to pieces, never to be allowed to live again. I cut it off of my life, in Jesus' name. Father, I take my Sword, Your Word, and I cut off the head of the spirit of disobedience in my life. Lord, I cut it off my life now, in Jesus' Name, I hack it to pieces, Lord so that there is no breath or life in it. Holy Spirit, come fill me now. Jesus, breathe on me anew. Fill me with breath and spirit, Your breath and Spirit. Thank you Jesus."

Amen.

EDIE BAYER

Ephesians 5:22-24 (ESV)

Wives, submit to your own husbands, as to the Lord. For the husband is the head of the wife even as Christ is the head of the church, his body, and is himself its Savior. Now as the church submits to Christ, so also wives should submit in everything to their husbands.

The fifth Power Thief is a spirit of Unsubmissiveness.

The submissive attitude specified by God is summed up here in the husband and wife relationship. However, it is a universal attitude that the Father would have us live with, with everyone everywhere:

"Submit to one another out of reverence for Christ." (Eph. 5:21, NIV)

That means everyone submit to one another. That we all submit to our leaders, and that our leaders submit to Christ.

In a perfect world. But we live in a fallen world.

That doesn't stop us from trying to conform to the image of Christ, just that we have a few members of our group that really don't LIKE to submit. I dare say that a bunch of folks don't like to do it. Everyone wants to be the leader, and no one wants to do the work. Everyone wants to be in charge and no one wants to be held accountable.

I was watching a T.D. Jakes video one time, and I think he said it best, "Everybody wants what T.D. Jakes has, but nobody wants to go through what T.D. Jakes went through to get it!"

We could say that about anyone that is in a position of authority. Ask most Christian speakers today what their testimony is, where they came from, what they went through to get on the platform and speaking in front of the microphone. Most of them went through undiluted HELL to get on the platform. Most of the young speakers today, today's evangelists, went through Drug Addiction and satanic attacks and overdoses and heart failures and demonic possession to get on the platform. Some of them woke up in a ditch somewhere. Imagine all the ones that never woke up! The next generation of evangelists had to go through a lot to be "real", to have a testimony to reach the young people of today.

And still, nobody wants to submit.

The Bible is very clear on this point as well, that we should submit to authority, because everyone who is placed in a position of power is set there by God. He didn't ask you if it made you happy. He put that person in a position to accomplish His own purposes, although sometimes that may line up with yours. Now, it might make you happy to have a Republican in office and make you unhappy to have a Democrat. The Israelites didn't get a vote on whether or not the Romans took control. The Chaldeans were used by the Lord as a tool of chastisement, as were the Babylonians. Later the Egyptians were used to showcase the Glory of God. But the Israelites never had a say-so in the placement of these authorities into their lives. They were required to submit to them. Period.

In fact, the Lord says in Jer. 29:7, NIV, "Also, seek the peace and prosperity of the city to which I have carried you into exile. Pray to the LORD for it, because if it prospers, you too will prosper." Not only were they required to submit to these authorities, they were required to pray for the captors.

Really, PRAY for them? Yes.

There was no option to be unsubmissive. As slaves in Egypt, they had to submit to Pharaoh and his taskmasters. Later, they had to submit to Moses, and then later still to men appointed by Moses and his father-in-law. Then they had to submit to Judges, then to Kings. They were always required to submit to somebody, somewhere – some form of authority.

And so are we. Whether we want to or not, we are called to submit. One to another and to authority, we are required to submit. When we do not, we are in rebellion. (Please read that chapter again if you have any questions about that fruit!)

There is a spirit, an unsubmissive spirit, which is in close association with the spirits of rebellion, disobedience and pride and works VERY closely with the Jezebel spirit. If you have found yourself bucking authority, doing what you want to do instead of submitting to what you have been asked to do, and kicking against the goads, you may have it. I sure have!

I have struggled for the last several years to overcome the spirit of unsubmissiveness. I was a single mother for 5-years before getting married to Darryl, so I was IT -- mother and father, breadwinner and housewife, cleaning lady, doctor and handyman. I had to play all the roles. There was an old TV commercial where a housewife is standing in her business suit with a frying pan in her hand, while she sings "I bring home the bacon and fry it up in a pan". That was me!

Before that I was married to my son's father and I was the head of the household, because that was the way that I was raised, with the woman in charge. Even worse, as time went by I made so much money that I advised my son's father to quit working! Wow, talk about identity theft! Then I was REALLY in control. The Jezebel spirit had free rein in my household.

That is a FAR CRY from how the Bible says it should be. We should be equals, with the woman submitting to the man when it comes to all decisions since the man is supposed to be praying to get his directions from God. In truthfulness, there should be no disagreements, if both parties are praying and hearing from the Lord, since He will tell both people the same thing.

I know firsthand that it is really HARD to change, even when it is required by God. It's hard to trust somebody else with decisions that affect your life on every level. Now, keep in mind, God knows your heart. He knows if you are trying and really want to be obedient. But obedience is crucial, and one of the rules of the Kingdom of God is the woman MUST submit to the man.

There cannot be two heads in a marriage, two people both vying to control the relationship. I heard a Pastor say, "Anything with two heads is not natural and needs to die!" That means the man is the head and the woman is not.

Sorry girls.

The key is that the man MUST submit to God. If he is not asking for direction from the Lord, the two are lost.

And that is where I believe that most married couples have their issues. Everyone knows that there are more women in church than men. Do we still take our directives from a husband who is not walking with God? The answer is yes, unless he asks you to do something illegal or immoral.

I know many women have had issues in the "trust zone". They do not trust that their husband ALWAYS hears from God on every occasion, sometimes if at all. They are most likely correct. However, their job is NOT TO JUDGE. God may be speaking to the man in a way that the man "hears" him, even without recognizing His voice. Many women are not sure that their husband even ASKS God for His input. I know I've been there!

I hear from God, too. It just seems that Darryl and I hear different things all the time, and I am still required to submit to Darryl's decisions. My husband uses "logic" a lot, because that is how he is built. Most of what God does is totally illogical, to quote Mr. Spock. So Darryl will do what he thinks is right, and that scares me. Doing something completely illogical does not!

But our role is to support our husbands. Be a Proverbs 31 woman. Respect him, honor him, take care of him. That is our role. To be the neck and support the head. After all, our children are to submit to us, right? Our employees are to submit to us, right? The church congregation is to submit one to another, and then to the leadership, right?

It is to be the same in ministry. Submit to authority. Unquestioningly. Assume that the ministry head hears from God (even if their actions do not show that they are asking Him anything at all). It is not your job to judge the minister. It is your job to submit to their authority and carry out their instructions.

I had a conversation with a Pastor one time about submission. The Pastor with whom I was speaking was asking me how I could submit to another minister so unquestioningly. I said it was my job to submit, not to judge. It was their ministry, and they had to be accountable to God for their decisions. My job was to submit, and not to question. God did not put me in control (or at the head) of that ministry. If He wanted me to run the ministry, He would have made me ministry head. As it was, I was not, so my job was to submit. Submit without question, carry out orders and instructions to the best of my abilities, ask for help when I need it, delegate when authorized to do so, and do nothing without permission. That is the rule of ministry. It's very simple, and VERY EGO SMASHING. Which is as it should be.

Now if I could just translate that into my marriage!

My sister and I used to work together in high school as waitresses at the same coffee shop. She was told to do something one time by management. She started to tell him what she thought they ought to do instead. He told her, "I don't pay you to THINK, I pay you to WORK!"

In essence, THAT is submission. Even if what the person in authority is doing makes no sense to you, your job is to WORK (submit), not to THINK (not submit). (Unless they pay you to be in a think-tank, and of course, your boss would never say something like that to begin with!) Whether you are a son or a daughter, an employee or a ministry associate, a wife or a citizen of some country somewhere, you MUST BE SUBMITTED to someone. In fact, BEING SUBMITTED is a work in progress. We are surely not born that way!

We have a boarder staying in one of our rooms right now. He's a nice guy who walks with the Lord. He has been with us for several months now while the pipeline is going in through Houston. I walked through the living room one day, and the letters for the word "BELIEVE" were rearranged on my coffee table to say "BE LIVE". The "E" was double stacked and there was a space in between, so it looked like two words, "Be" and "Live". Personally I have always thought that there should be an "A" in there somewhere so we could rearrange it to say "BE ALIVE"!

I looked at that, and thought our wild Canadian prophet friend Darren Canning had done it, since he always stays with us here when he is in town and he had just left to go back to Canada on Sunday.

I smiled and walked off, and the next day I changed the letters back to "BELIEVE".

The gentleman who is renting the room, our boarder, said to me yesterday, "I noticed you changed the letters back to 'BELIEVE'." He went on to say, "I think that people should BE and LIVE. We are human BEINGS and not human DOINGS! We spend too much time DOING and not enough time BEING."

Jesus says in John 10:10 that He came to give us LIFE and LIFE MORE ABUNDANTLY. That means that we are to LIVE according to the Father's standards for the rules of engagement. I agree to a certain extent with what my boarder said, that we spend way too much time "doing" and not enough time "being".

We have to BE what the Father created us to be, in His image. We must submit one to another, and all of us submit to God. That is TRULY LIVING.

Turn Your Power On, Shut Down the Power Thief "Unsubmissiveness" – Key #5

Ask God for forgiveness. 1 John 1:9

If we confess our sins, he is faithful and just to forgive us *our* sins, and to cleanse us from all unrighteousness.

Repent of your involvement with the spirit of Rebellion. Acts 3:19

So repent (change your mind and purpose); turn around *and* return [to God], that your sins may be erased (blotted out, wiped clean), that times of refreshing (of recovering from the effects of heat, of [a]reviving with fresh air) may come from the presence of the Lord;

1. Repent of your involvement with the spirit of unsubmissiveness
2. Repent to your husband (fiancé, parents, Pastor, employer or other) of not submitting and ask for their forgiveness
3. Ask God for Forgiveness
4. Ask Holy Spirit to come in and fill you up
5. Revel in your freedom from the bondage of being in control! (It's all an illusion!)

Prayer: "Father forgive me for not submitting to the authority that you have set into position over my life. Forgive me for not trusting you to know what you are doing! Lord, in Jesus' Name I repent of my involvement with the unsubmissive spirit. Father I have repented to (_____) for not submitting to his/her authority. Lord, thank you for both your forgiveness and theirs. Holy Spirit, come now and fill me up. Lord, I thank you for the authority figures you have given to me to whom I must submit. I will submit to these and any others you place in my life, for I know that all authority stems from you. Father, I know that with the same measure that I submit to authority will authority be granted unto me. Thank you for your generous gift of authority to me in my life. Thank you Jesus!"

Matthew 7:1-5

Amplified Bible (AMP)

7 Do not judge *and* criticize *and* condemn others, so that you may not be judged *and* criticized *and* condemned yourselves.

2 For just as you judge *and* criticize *and* condemn others, you will be judged *and* criticized *and* condemned, and in accordance with the measure you [use to] deal out to others, it will be dealt out again to you.

3 Why do you [a]stare from without at the [b]very small particle that is in your brother's eye but do not become aware of *and* consider the beam [c]of timber that is in your own eye?

4 Or how can you say to your brother, Let me get the tiny particle out of your eye, when there is the beam [d]of timber in your own eye?

5 You hypocrite, first get the beam of timber out of your own eye, and then you will see clearly to take the tiny particle out of your brother's eye.

The sixth Power Thief is a Judgmental or a Critical Spirit.

I heard recently that we judge other people by their actions, but we want to be judged by our INTENT. So typically human! I am glad that God is not like us.

It seems like fault finding, judging other people's actions and being hyper-critical are some of the easiest things for us to do as human beings. They seem to come naturally to us. But Jesus told us not to judge "lest you be judged" (Matt. 7:1, NASB). If we judge others, when we criticize and find fault in others, we are in agreement with the enemy. This gives him power and he doesn't need our help!

There is a critical and judgmental spirit in operation all throughout the Bible. In the Old Testament, Sarai criticized her maid Hagar out of jealousy after Ishmael was born (Gen 16:1, 9-10). Could it be that she felt she had lost her position of power once Ishmael was born, and that Hagar could become her equal? She certainly voiced it to Abram,
9 "Now Sarai saw the son of Hagar the Egyptian, whom she had borne to Abram, mocking [Isaac].

10 Therefore she said to Abram, Cast out this bondwoman and her son, for the son of this bondwoman shall not be an heir with my son Isaac."

Surprisingly, God allowed Abram to kick Hagar out, drawing a line in the sand for all time between Isaac and Ishmael, between Judaism and Islam. It was clear cut distinction then, and is still the same today.

In 1 Samuel Chapter 1 and 2, the prophet Samuel's mother Hannah had a problem with his father's second wife. This woman was Hannah's rival, named Peninnah. There are no scripture quotes as to what Peninnah actually said, but scripture records that she "provoked" Hannah deliberately. She likely mocked her, criticized her and definitely judged herself as better than Hannah because Peninnah had children and Hannah did not. Everyone knows that in that time period children were counted as wealth, and the more children one had, the richer one was. Her behavior, however, was the fruit of jealousy, because her husband – the same man as Hannah's husband—favored Hannah more and gave her double portions of food, more than he gave to Peninnah and her children. Again, I believe that it was jealousy rooted in insecurity, fearing that her position of power, and her children's well-being and security, was threatened by Hannah.

In King Hezekiah's day, during his reign in 2 Kings 29, we see the critical spirit again. This is definitely a "power play" between good and evil, between God and the enemy! This time the Assyrian king sent his cupbearer, Rabshakeh, to deliver a message on his behalf to King Hezekiah, intending to intimidate him and the Jews. He had wrongly judged their Big "G" God as being on the same level as all their other little "g" gods of their region. His critical spirit showed up when he did, at the wall where Hezekiah's men were, on the road to the fuller's field.

He started off by criticizing Hezekiah, "^{29} Thus says the king: Let not Hezekiah deceive you. For he will not be able to deliver you out of my hand."

Then he stepped up the criticism and judgments another level, and started in on God! He said, "^{30} Nor let Hezekiah make you trust in *and* rely on the Lord, saying, The Lord will surely deliver us, and this city will not be given into the hand of Assyria's king.

^{31} Hearken not to Hezekiah, for thus says the king of Assyria: Make your peace with me and come out to me, and eat every man from his own vine and fig tree and drink every man the waters of his own cistern,

^{32} Until I come and take you away to a land like your own, a land of grain and vintage fruit, of bread and vineyards, of olive trees and honey, that you may live and not die. Do not listen to Hezekiah when he urges you, saying, The Lord will deliver us.

^{33} Has any one of the gods of the nations ever delivered his land out of the hand of the king of Assyria?

^{34} Where are the gods of Hamath and Arpad [in Syria]? Where are the gods of Sepharvaim, Hena, and Ivvah [in the Euphrates Valley]? Have they delivered Samaria [Israel's capital] out of my hand?

^{35} Who of all the gods of the countries has delivered his country out of my hand, that the Lord should deliver Jerusalem out of my hand?" (2 Kings 29-35, Amp.)

Scripture shows in several different places including Isaiah 36 that this Assyrian king's army gets defeated and he actually ends up getting murdered by his own sons for voicing his arrogance and blaspheming the Holy One of Israel. God doesn't like that at all!

Jesus faced judgment and this same critical spirit head on with the Pharisees and the Herodians in all the Gospels. However, Jesus Himself never had a judgmental or critical attitude toward anyone other than the Pharisees and the other hypocritical religious leaders of that time, including a couple of scribes. He never criticized anyone, not one person, even when the Jews were ignorant, vicious or downright blasphemous to him, even Judas!

Jesus explained why a judgmental attitude is so dangerous: "God will be as hard on you as you are on others! He will treat you exactly as you treat them" (v.2). When we judge, we invite judgment upon ourselves. The Bible says that "...judgment will be merciless to one who has shown no mercy" (James 2:13). We reap what we sow. I need to reap MERCY! I certainly don't need to reap any more judgment. How about you?

This is where it gets personal for me. I used to pride myself on having no mercy. Enough said!

I would jokingly laugh that I skipped the mercy line; that I preferred to fillet people, rip their guts out, reach into their innards to rip the problem out and and shove it in their face; they would come to me with a problem and I would slice them open, pull the problem out and show it to them; I never got a "mercy bone", and other such sayings.

However, that was just a "cover-up" for a judgmental spirit. It was easier for me to judge others if I "said" I didn't have any mercy. I didn't realize this at the time, of course, it was not intentional. I was just infected with the two twin sisters – judgmental spirit and critical spirit. I consistently judged other people by my own standards, and I was consistently critical when they didn't meet them.

God loved me too much to leave me like that! He needed me to have a heart for where He is sending me. And He needs YOU to have a heart also, because He has big plans for you!

I'd be on the phone answering prayer calls, listening to someone who desperately needed a word from the Word. I'd be asking them, "Do you have a Bible in your house? Come on, knock the cobwebs off of it!" or "Do you tithe? The Yes and Amen promises of God are for TITHERS!" I was judge and jury all in one.

But God.

Beginning even then God was already at work in my life, trying to dig the mercy out of the deep place that I had buried it.

In fact, one day, one of the other ministry associates got a phone call that made her completely break down crying. She was crying and trying to tell me what the call was about, and the spirit of weeping was so heavy that I started to cry too, just from her telling me about the prayer call. She was so broken up she needed to go home, so I agreed to talk to our office manager for her. I started to tell him about the call she got, and I started crying all over again. Sobbing, I told him, "Her mercy got all over me!" and I was brushing my arms, as if I was trying to wipe it off. He laughed and laughed at me! But she got to go home. And God was at work.

In my first book, "Spiritual Espionage", God sent me on a spiritual journey to take back ground that the enemy had stolen. Along the way, I learned a few things. He allowed me to find mercy in places that I never would have voluntarily gone, had He not sent me. In one of these places, I met a lady who had been traumatized by the death of her brother by stroke. It put such a spirit of fear into her life it had a stronghold over her. Soon afterward she had a stroke herself, and was convinced that she was going to die of a stroke just like her brother.

God deliberately placed her in my path, knowing that I would pray for her to help her rid her life of the spirits of fear and trauma, and cut off the generational curses in her life. I cannot honestly say that she was healed of her stroke, although she may be totally healed, but I can say for sure that the spirits of fear and trauma left her on the spot! She was so much better when we were done praying it was amazing. And I found a mercy bone.

In addition to her healing, I got healed --- of a judgmental spirit! The Lord sat me down and had me document every step of the journey in "Spiritual Espionage". I realized along the way that He was working in me. God is so good that way.

"Always be humble and gentle. Patiently put up with each other and love each other. Try your best to let God's Spirit keep your hearts united. Do this by living in peace" (Eph. 4:2,3).

Turn Your Power On, Shut Down the Power Thief "Judgmental / Critical Spirit" – Key #6

Ask God for forgiveness. 1 John 1:9

If we confess our sins, he is faithful and just to forgive us *our* sins, and to cleanse us from all unrighteousness.

Repent of having a judgmental / critical spirit. Acts 3:19

So repent (change your mind and purpose); turn around *and* return [to God], that your sins may be erased (blotted out, wiped clean), that times of refreshing (of recovering from the effects of heat, of [a]reviving with fresh air) may come from the presence of the Lord;

Command the judgmental and critical spirits to go.
10:17

Then the seventy[c] returned with joy, saying, "Lord, even the demons are subject to us in Your name."

"Therefore encourage one another and build up one another." (1 Thess. 5:11)

"Brothers, if someone is caught in a sin, you who are spiritual should restore him gently." (Gal. 6:1)

The Keys to getting rid of a Critical or Judgmental Spirit:

1. Repent for coming into agreement with the Judgmental Spirit and the Critical Spirit.
2. Cut them off of your life.
3. Command them to go and to never return.
4. Ask Holy Spirit to fill up the places that these two spirits had previously occupied.
5. Now CHANGE YOUR MIND. You used to have a critical spirit and judge people harshly. You must put off the old man and renew your mind.

Prayer: "Lord, I repent for coming into agreement with the judgmental spirit and the critical spirit and for having any involvement with them. In the Name of Jesus I cut the judgmental spirit and the critical spirit off of my life. In the Name of Jesus I command the judgmental spirit and the critical spirit to go now and to never return. Lord, thank you that I build others up in love with my words and that I no longer sit in judgment of my brethren. Thank you Lord that I restore others back to you gently. Holy Spirit come fill me now, fill me up and fill up all the empty places that the judgmental spirit and the critical spirit had previously occupied. Jesus, breathe on me anew. Fill me with new life, with the ability to edify and exhort others building them up and no longer tearing them down, free of the judgmental spirit and the critical spirit. Thank you Jesus."

1 Samuel 15:22 Amplified

"Samuel said, 'Has the Lord as great a delight in burnt offerings and sacrifices as in obeying the voice of the Lord? Behold, to obey is better than sacrifice, and to hearken than the fat of rams.'"

The final Power Thief is Disobedience.

OBEDIENCE. It reminds us of when we were children, doesn't it? Remember when we were little we had to clean our rooms before we could go outside and play on Saturday morning -- "or else!" Just the very word alone stirs up images of painful sacrifice, doesn't it? Doesn't it make us think of doing things we don't want to do? Things like sitting still and not squirming, eating all our green vegetables and being quiet in the library, and no dessert unless we cleaned our plate.

Obedience is making somebody ELSE happy instead of yourself, right?

Whew. That would be awful...if it were true.

But this is God we are talking about, and He only wants what is best for you. He wants to keep you safe, chaste and holy. He wants to keep you out of the enemy's camp. He wants you to be in health and to prosper, even as your soul prospers (3 John 1:2). He has PLANS for you (Jer. 29:11) and He wants you to walk by His laws and His rules to accomplish those plans and purposes that He has predestined for your life (Romans 8:29).

In the Kingdom, Obedience is POWER.

The truth is obedience to the Lord is completely the opposite of awful. The enemy has pounded us our entire lifetimes to make us buy into his lie that "Obedience is bad, Rebellion is good!" We naturally are a rebellious people, so it is easy for us to gladly grasp onto the spirit of disobedience. We have been trained up excellently by the world, and once we are saved we usually we have to "un-learn" everything that we have learned in order to walk uprightly before the Lord.

In short, the world sells rebellion, but we cannot be buyers of it. The Lord requires obedience.

Obedience to the Lord is wonderful! Obedience relieves anxiety because you are no longer responsible for the outcome of your or anyone else's situation! Obedience to the Word of God gives freedom from worry and sleepless nights. Obedience releases us into the "new". Obedience upholds itself, because it will NEVER be wrong! God will never put you on the wrong path.

We need boundaries, and God's Word gives those to us. In addition, it is good to have a framework from which to operate. It is good to know right from wrong, but it is better to know right from "almost right"! I heard a Pastor preach once that if a person was "almost" saved, they were damned. It's not a "Oh well, close enough, maybe next time" scenario! Too many people think that what they are doing is right, but the Bible says, "There is a way which seems right to a man, but in the end it leads to death." (Proverbs 14:12, World English Bible). Only God's way leads to life...ETERNAL LIFE. Jesus came to give life, and life more abundantly (John 10:10). The thief (devil) only comes to steal, kill and destroy.

God would rather you be obedient than to sacrifice ANYTHING. Just say 'Yes' to Him, and say 'No' to the enemy. Anything that you hypothetically "give up" for Him will be returned back to you 100-fold *in this lifetime* (Mark 10:29-30). God knew that the things of the world would call to us when we give up the world for the Kingdom. That is why He says in Matthew 6:31, "Therefore do not worry *and* be anxious, saying, What are we going to have to eat? or, What are we going to have to drink? or, What are we going to have to wear?" He wants you to know that you will be rewarded NOW for your obedience to His will, and in the future, with life eternal (Mark 10:31).

Samuel gave the words of our flagship scripture, 1 Samuel 15:22, to Saul. He got them from another verse in the Old Testament, Isaiah 1:11:

> To what purpose is the multitude of your **sacrifice**s to Me [unless they are the offering of the heart]? says the Lord. I have had enough of the burnt offerings of rams and the fat of fed beasts [**without obedience**]; and I do not delight in the blood of bulls or of lambs or of he-goats [without righteousness] (Is. 1:11 Amp).

God doesn't want us to be pew-warmers, showing up on Sunday morning and as a Pastor I know would say, "...living like hell the rest of the week", doing as we please. Jesse Duplantis wrote a book about it, called, "What in Hell do you Want?" God doesn't want us to quit smoking and drinking, but keep on cussing and telling dirty jokes. He doesn't want us to steal at work but give at church, although that might appeal to some of you robin-hooders out there. He doesn't want us to go to the bars on Saturday nights and show up at church (maybe) on Sunday morning. He doesn't want us to be "CEO's" --- those that show up for worship on 'Christmas and Easter Only'. He doesn't want us to give up adultery to take up pornography, or vice versa (pardon the play on words!).

He doesn't want us to be partially obedient. He wants us to be fully obedient, all the way obedient --- all in. We cannot have the things of the world without keeping its king alive in us. We have to kill the king.

Continuing in Isaiah 1 v. 12, God says, "When you come to appear before Me, who requires of you that your [unholy feet] trample My courts?"

OUCH! Are you showing up in church because you WANT to, or because you HAVE to? If you are not there because you WANT to be in God's presence, exactly to whom are you being obedient? Who is making you go to church? Who is making you spend time in the presence of the Most High?

God wants us to be in relationship with Him and with Jesus. He doesn't want us to go to church faithfully but not have a RELATIONSHIP with Him. This requires obedience on our parts, discipline, too. He wants us to WANT to be obedient, to WANT to make Him happy. Faith requires obedience, and it is impossible to please the Lord without it. First you must believe that He IS, and then you must believe that He is a rewarder of those who diligently seek Him (Hebrews 11:6). So just to believe that He IS, you must FIRST be obedient to the Word of God and believe in God!

You can still do what you want to do. It's all about perception. Doing what you want to do is a matter of changing your tastes. "If you are willing and obedient, you shall eat the good of the land" (Is. 1:19 AMP). It's as easy as changing your menu. What do you want to eat?

I heard John Bevere teach about changing your appetite for food. He used to LOVE cheeseburgers and fries he said, but then started eating healthy. Eventually, he would reach for the fish instead of the cheeseburger when hungry.

Your spiritual appetite is the same. If you have a constant diet of "no church, no Word, no praise" that is what you will want to continue digesting. On the contrary, if you fill up continuously with "prayer, praise and fellowship", THAT is what you will crave! It is exactly the same with obedience to the Word of the Lord. Once you start following it for a while, you will follow it for LIFE, because only LIFE will satisfy you, since only He can fill up that Jesus-sized hole inside of you.

You will crave the good things that come with being obedient to the Word of your Father. It will please Him, and He will reward YOU. Don't you want to make your earthly Father happy, send him cards on Father's Day, take him out for dinner on his birthday? If you don't like your Dad and you do not have a good relationship with him, that's alright --- that's another topic and fodder for another message another time. I pray for healing in that relationship! There must be someone, certainly, that you want to please? What about your brother, your Mom, or your Pastor, your Husband, or your boyfriend (or girlfriend or your wife if you are a man)?

Making someone else happy is part of maturity, both spiritual and in the natural, and if it is GOD...well, the benefits FAR outweigh the costs. We are called to esteem others more highly than we do ourselves. That is so alien in our culture, which is a "me, Me, ME!" mentality. There is no way that we can do anything but esteem Him more highly than ourselves, once we taste and see that the Lord is good. Once you know Him, you want to know Him more, and when you draw closer to God, He draws closer to you. You will want to do whatever it takes to please Him, because only that will please you.

We are an instant gratification nation. We want it, and we want it NOW, make ME feel good NOW, fix me NOW. But His is an upside down Kingdom, and we must wait for our rewards. They come at His feet, serving Him and waiting upon Him, out of obedience. Obedience in the Kingdom is POWER.

I could fill up an entire library with instances of my own personal disobedience. In fact, it's shocking actually that not only am I still alive, but I am preaching the Gospel! I am alive because of Him, for Him, because He has a plan, and His plan includes me. Hopefully it also includes preaching and writing books, because I sure do like it!

I started telling a story about my ex-husband, my son's father. Allow me to finish. In 2007 we were making plans to attempt to reconcile (yet again!), this time in Colorado. We had been divorced for three years already, so I had three years of earnest renewal and seriously walking with Jesus in me. Anyway, all three of us moved to Colorado, west of Glenwood Springs. After a very short time, perhaps only two or three months, I realized it was a terrible mistake. I started praying for a way out of the mess that I had gotten us into.

Honestly, before we got back together, I was in the Word, and the Lord had already told me, "Do not go back in time, go forward." I wrote it in my bible the day He said it. I didn't realize it applied to this relationship! I thought it had to do with letting go of the past, making amends, reconciling my marriage and so forth.

Now we were back in Colorado and I was praying, HARD! The Lord told me I had the Spirit of Wisdom, and the Spirit of Revelation Knowledge. He honored the fact that I was trying to uphold my covenant with Him by attempting to reconcile with my son's father. However, He wanted me to move back to Texas.

So, here I was in Colorado. No car. No money. No way to get out of the condo we were in. Certainly no way to get back to Texas.

BUT GOD.

The Lord introduced me to some folks at the church I was attending in Colorado who were quite well-to-do. They offered to let me and my son stay with them at their beautiful home in the mountains, which we did, in an amazing mother-in-law suite complete with a super-huge TV and a gorgeous view. They loaned me a car to drive. They fed us, my son even played their piano, and I was able to work online and use their phone for business for a while. I ministered to the woman who was full of demons, but wanted to get free, and she did! She ended up giving me her Bible (which I still have, a King James).

So now my son and I were out of the condo, but I still didn't have any way to get back to Texas.

BUT GOD.

He put it on a friend of mine's heart to give me the money to rent a UHaul to get home. I didn't have to ask her, she volunteered because she wanted me to come home! I didn't have a vehicle to pull the trailer, so she loaned me enough to rent a truck. Thankfully I didn't need it, because my son's father ended up getting pulled over for a missing tail light cover, resulting in another DWI. He wasn't able to drive his truck. He loaned it to me, so I could pull the UHaul trailer back to Texas. I had to promise to get the truck back to him in Colorado.

The disobedience part is this: God told me not to get back together with my son's father, not to go backwards in time but rather to move forward. I was disobedient, I guess ignorantly, which may have been my saving grace. The Lord still fixed everything, orchestrated it all! I didn't do any of it. He arranged the place to stay, the money from my friend, even got me the truck from my ex-husband through the DWI.

God took care of everything – because I was obedient to do what He said to do.

However, I didn't willingly give the truck back to my son's father. I should have because that was the agreement. But I had decided he owed me that truck for back child support. Of course, he did not agree. He came out from Colorado and took the truck from my driveway in the pre-dawn hours.

He didn't even have to break into it. He had another set of keys, so he just started it up and drove away.

But God fixes everything. He makes all things new. He gave me an old Chevy Astro van, "La Bomba" we called it because it needed transmission fluid AND oil, every day. It had no defroster and no heat and no air conditioning. I had to take jars of hot water out and pour them on the windshield to take my son to school and both of us bundle up in blankets for the drive. But after no vehicle to drive for a few weeks I was grateful to have it!

Until He gave me the 2000 F150 pickup. Now THERE'S a God Story.

That story will be in my next book! Then He gave me a God-fearing husband, and a great house. And a wonderful ministry and good friends.

The Abundant Life that He promised in John 10:10. Is it perfect and trouble free? NO. He never promised that. He only said that He would give us LIFE, and LIFE MORE ABUNDANTLY. And He has.

Here is the real reason you want to be obedient to the Word of God:

21 The person who has My commands and keeps them is the one who [really] loves Me; and whoever [really] loves Me will be loved by My Father, and I [too] will love him and will show (reveal, manifest) Myself to him. [I will let Myself be clearly seen by him and make Myself real to him.]

22 Judas, not Iscariot, asked Him, Lord, how is it that You will reveal Yourself [make Yourself real] to us and not to the world?

23 Jesus answered, If a person [really] loves Me, he will keep My word [obey My teaching]; and My Father will love him, and We will come to him and make Our home (abode, special dwelling place) with him. **(John 14:21-23** AMP)

Obedience is Power. We want His Miracle-Working Power, in our own lives and to testify to others. We WANT to obey God because we want Him to come and make Himself manifest to us, for others. We WANT God to be real to us, and to make Him real to others. We WANT to walk with Him in the cool of the day, and we WANT Him there in the heat of the battle! We want God to be with us, and not against us. We want God to fight FOR us and not fight against us. We want Him to command the blessing to come upon us and bless all the works of our hands. We want Him to take care of us and protect us.

We WANT Him to justify us. Because we cannot justify ourselves.

OBEDIENCE truly is the POWER. Holy Ghost Power. Healing, Saving

Power. Sons and daughters of God POWER. Manifest, Miracle-Working Power. When you obey God He will do everything to make sure that He shows up in your life. That is TRUE POWER.

Walking with God can only be done through accepting Jesus Christ as your Lord and Savior. Have you done that? Are you SURE?

Don't take any chances. Read this out loud, and be SURE that you are saved!

"Dear Lord Jesus,

I know I am a sinner, and I ask for your forgiveness. I believe you died for my sins and rose from the dead. I trust and follow you as my Lord and Savior. Guide my life and help me to do your will.

In your name, amen."

And now, be OBEDIENT. Have FAITH. The Power flows from Obedience to the Will and the Works of God. When you hear Him, obey Him and believe by Faith, because without FAITH it is impossible to please God. Even if it doesn't make sense, even if it goes completely against every grain of your personality and makes your skin crawl and the hair on your neck stand on end....do it.

Give these spirits the boot and you will be Turning Up Your Power!!

Prayer: Dear Jesus, in Your Name I pray! I am calling things that are not as those they truly were, Lord Jesus. I decree that I have Your commands and I am keeping them because I really love You! Jesus, because I really love you, I will be loved by the Father, and you will love me and make Yourself manifest to me. Lord, because I love you, I will keep Your Word and obey Your teaching, and the Father will love me and You both will come to me and make Your home and special dwelling place with me! Lord, when I am obedient to You I shut down the power of darkness. Help me to continue to be obedient to Your Will and Your Way! Jesus, I want to manifest Your Miracle Working Power! I am saved and born again, a disciple walking with You. Come to me and make Yourself Real to me so that I can make You real to those that you have given to me, and so that Your Miracles, Signs and Wonders will follow me wherever I go. For Your Glory God, for Your Kingdom I pray. Amen!

Power Thieves

ABOUT THE AUTHOR

Edie Bayer's primary focus is to promote and advance the Kingdom of God by helping people to hear and recognize the voice of the Lord, and then act upon it. Edie has served with international ministers Joan Hunter and Paulette Reed as well as Darren Canning and Dr. Judy Laird. Edie ministers as a Preacher and Prophet of God. She is an author, a speaker and itinerant minister.

Edie and her husband Darryl formed Kingdom Promoters (www.KingdomPromoters.org), to help further God's Kingdom by acting as an incubator to assist fledgling ministries in their start-up stages. Kingdom Promoters also hosts itinerant speakers and travelling ministers such as Dr. Linda Smith and Apostle William Dillon, as well as author Carol Sewell, among others.

Edie and Darryl reside on a small homestead north of the Houston area. They raise chickens, ducks, quail and rabbits and have three cats.

9 780692 211151